Five Senses
Phonics

BOOK 4

Hunter Calder

A
FIVE SENSES
PUBLICATION

Five Senses Education Pty Ltd
2/195 Prospect Highway
Seven Hills NSW 2147 Australia
Phone   02 838 9265
Email   sevenhills@fivesenseseducation.com.au
Web   www.fivesenseseducation.com.au

Calder, Hunter
Five Senses Phonics Book 4
978-1-76032-425-4

2022 10 18

Contents

About the Author

Multiple award-winning author Hunter Calder has extensive experience as a reading teacher, consultant, teacher trainer and lecturer, both in Australia and overseas. He obtained a Master of Arts from the University of Sydney and a Master of Education from the University of New South Wales. His many publications include the acclaimed *Reading Freedom 2000* series and the *Excel Basic English* books. He also contributed to the *Literacy Planet* online program.

The *Five Senses Phonics Series* of early literacy skills is his most recent series of phonics books and is the outcome of collaboration with the experienced people at Five Senses Education.

Introduction

Welcome to *Five Senses Phonics*, a carefully structured series of activity books for pre-readers and beginning readers at the important stage of their literacy acquisition. The Five Senses activity books are intended for use in a preschool setting, in the beginning school years, and for older students who are having difficulty learning to read.

Book 4 continues the development of essential reading skills — basic phonics. Phonics applies a student's ability to hear and work with sounds in spoken words to reading them on the page. At this stage students work with initial and terminal blends to read them into words. They learn, for instance, that the sounds 'st' - 'a' - 'nd' blend together to form the word 'stand'. Contemporary research tells us that students with good phonics skills go on to become competent readers. On the other hand, preschool age children and students in the early years at school who do not understand the relationship between spoken and written words are likely to develop literacy problems. Students who experience difficulty learning the skills of phonics may need the services of a specialised teacher trained in the development of auditory perception techniques.

The exercises are structured to allow the student to progressively attain competence when reading words containing initial and terminal blends. Students then progress to Book 5 to work with more advanced phonics skills – consonant digraphs ('sh', 'ch' 'th' and so on), long vowel rules ('a' as in 'rain' and 'a' as in 'gate') and words containing the soft 'c' and 'g' sounds ('cent' and 'page').

Student progress should regularly be monitored and evaluated after completing each level, using the Achievement Tests section which is specifically designed for teachers to assess effectiveness and so students can see the positive results of their learning experiences.

Instructions for Book 4

Note: Each unit of work in Book 4 follows the same procedure and maintains the same format.

Pages 1–5	**Vowel and consonant sounds** — teach these sounds carefully and until students can reproduce them automatically.
Pages 6–11	**Basic Sight Vocabulary** — these lists contain the basic sight words students need to work successfully with the program. Teach the words list by list until they are mastered, and once they are mastered regularly revise them. The basic sight words are presented at the bottom of each page so students can learn or revise them as they progress through the book.
Page 12	Teach students the terminal blends on this page ('nd' as in 'hand' and so on). The words they are learning in this unit (except the sight words) contain these blends and the single letter-sound correspondences learned in the earlier levels.
Pages 13–24	Students complete the activity pages that teach them to work and read terminal blends.
Page 25	Students display competence reading words containing terminal blends.
Page 26	Teach students the initial blends on this page ('fl' as in 'flag'and so on). The words they learn in this unit (except the sight words) contain these blends and the single letter-sound correspondences learned in the earlier levels.
Page 27–38	Students complete the activity pages that teach them to work and read initial blends.
Page 39	Students display competence reading words containing initial blends.
Page 40	Teach students the initial blends on this page ('st' as in 'stamp' and so on). The words they learn in this unit (except the sight words) contain these blends and the single letter-sound correspondences learned in the earlier levels.
Page 41–52	Students complete the activity pages that teach them to work and read initial blends.

Sound Charts

Single Letter-Sound Correspondences: Vowels

Say the sounds for these letters.

a   as   in

e   as   in

i   as   in

o   as   in

u   as   in

Sound Charts   Single Letter-Sound Correspondences: Consonants

Say the sounds for these letters.

b   as   in

c   as   in

d   as   in

f   as   in

g   as   in

Sound Charts

Single Letter-Sound Correspondences: Consonants

Say the sounds for these letters.

h as in

j as in

k as in

l as in

m as in

Sound Charts

Say the sounds for these letters.

n   as   in

p   as   in

r   as   in

s   as   in

t   as   in

Sound Charts

Single Letter-Sound Correspondences: Consonants

Say the sounds for these letters.

V   as   in

W   as   in

x   as   in

y   as   in

z   as   in

Basic Sight Vocabulary

Learn these lists of sight words

a	in	and	saw	into	this
am	is	are	she	play	what
as	it	for	the	said	when
by	Mr	her	too	then	will
he	no	him	was	they	with
if	of	Mrs	why		
	on	not	yes		
		out	you		

Basic Sight Vocabulary

Can I read these words?

List One		List Two	
and	look	at	man
are	my	away	me
boy	of	big	not
can	play	blue	on
come	red	down	one
funny	run	for	ran
go	said	good	saw
he	says	green	three
is	see	have	too
jump	the	here	up
like	this	in	watch
little	to	it	you

☐/12 ☐/12 ☐/12 ☐/12

Yes I can!

Sight Words 3

Basic Sight Vocabulary

Can I read these words?

List Three		List Four	
all	going	an	had
am	home	after	help
around	into	as	her
black	make	be	him
but	no	brown	his
by	old	cold	if
call	out	did	she
came	was	ever	some
do	we	fly	stop
eat	will	from	two
fast	yellow	girl	who
get	yes	give	woman

[/12]   [/12]   [/12]   [/12]

Yes I can!

8

Sight Words 4

Basic Sight Vocabulary

Can I read these words?

List Five		List Six	
above	new	about	how
find	now	again	long
gave	over	always	or
got	put	any	them
has	round	ask	then
Its	school	ate	they
know	so	cannot	walk
let	soon	could	went
live	ten	does	were
made	that	father	what
many	under	first	when
may	your	found	with

☐/12   ☐/12   ☐/12   ☐/12

Yes I can!

Sight Words 5

Basic Sight Vocabulary

Can I read these words?

List Seven		List Eight	
because	once	brother	pull
Been	open	buy	show
Before	our	draw	sit
bring	say	drink	small
children	take	even	their
done	tell	fall	these
every	there	grow	think
goes	upon	hold	those
mother	us	hot	very
much	want	just	where
must	wish	keep	which
never	would	only	work

☐ /12   ☐ /12   ☐ /12   ☐ /12

Yes I can!

10

Sight Words 6

Basic Sight Vocabulary

Can I read these words?

List Nine		List Ten	
best	pick	baby	Sing
better	please	daughter	sister
both	pretty	far	sleep
clean	read	house	something
cut	shall	hurt	son
eight	six	kind	start
five	today	laugh	thank
four	try	Mr	together
full	use	Mrs	warm
light	well	Own	wash
myself	why	right	water
off	wrtte	seven	white

☐/12   ☐/12   ☐/12   ☐/12

Yes I can!

Say the sounds for these blends.

nd as in	sk as in
mp as in	lt as in
nt as in	lk as in
st as in	ft as in

and   are   boy

Circle the picture with the blend.

can   come   funny   (13)

Circle the picture with the blend.

go   he   is   jump

Draw a line to the blend the picture ends with.

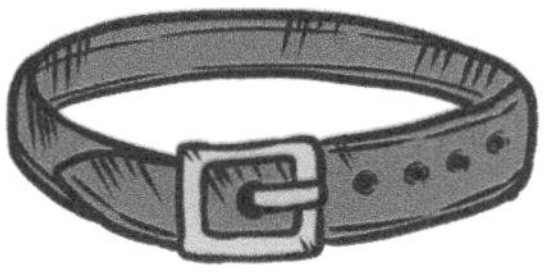

nd
mp
lt

lk
st
ft

sk
lt
lk

nd
mp
nt

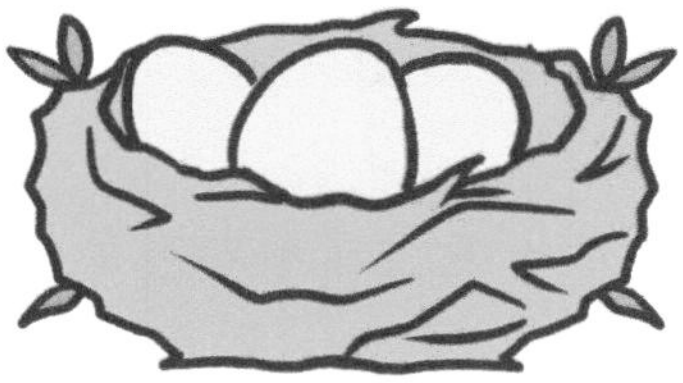

st
nt
mp

nt
st
ft

ft
nd
lk

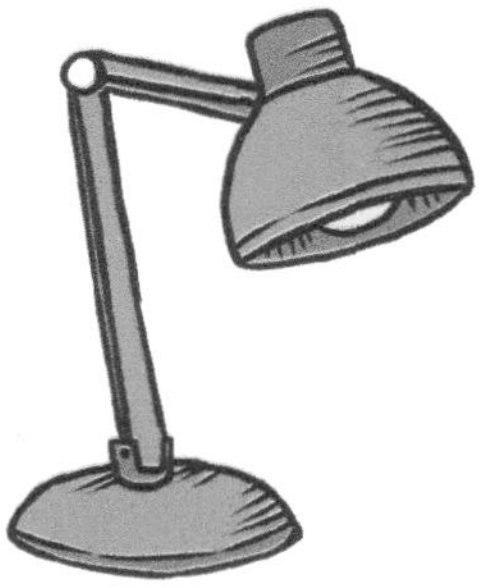

lt
sk
mp

like   little   look   my   (15)

Circle the blend the picture ends with.

nd mp sk	lk st ft
lt lk ft	nd mp nt
st mp lt	nt st ft
nd lk sk	nd sk mp

(16)   of   play   red   run

Write the missing letters.

la ___ ___ ___	te ___ ___	ha ___ ___ ___
ve ___ ___	be ___ ___ ___	ma ___ ___ ___

Underline the word for the picture

1. help   past   tusk   hunt

2. mend   milk   hint   rust

3. ant   soft   list   bump

4. dust   next   cost   fist

5. lift   sand   nest   wind

said   says   see   the   (17)

Write the missing letters.

tu _ _ _

ca _ _ _

a _ _ _

de _ _ _

le _ _ _

sa _ _ _

wi _ _ _

po _ _ _

mi _ _ _

du _ _ _

pa _ _ _

re _ _ _

Draw a line to match the words that rhyme.

band	lend	cast	lift
end	pump	mask	fond
lump	damp	gift	past
camp	sand	pond	task

Circle the word for the picture.

band bands	desks desk
lamps lamp	tent tents

List the words with the same word pattern
under each picture.

rest   sand   cask   land   west

band   bask   pest   task

_____	_____	_____

Unit 1:9

Draw a line from the picture to the matching word.

fist
list
mist

sand
band
land

rest
best
vest

lift
gift
sift

Write the word that fits in the word shape box.

milk	soft	best
bond	mist	lamp
wept	help	past
limp	hilt	pump

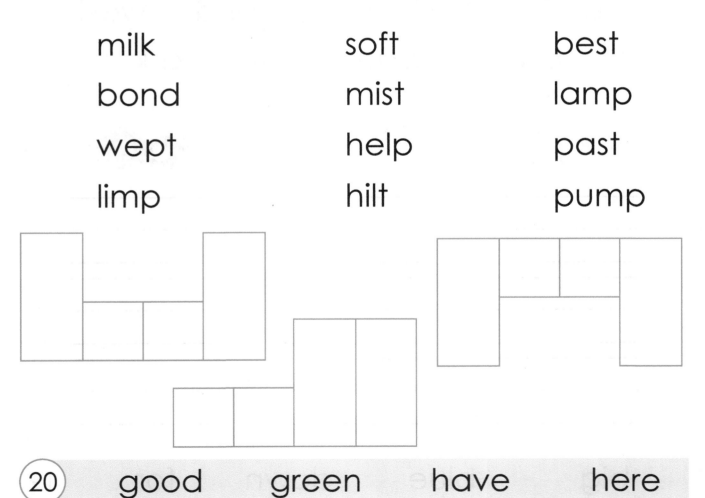

20 good   green   have   here

Unit 1:10

Write the words for the pictures.

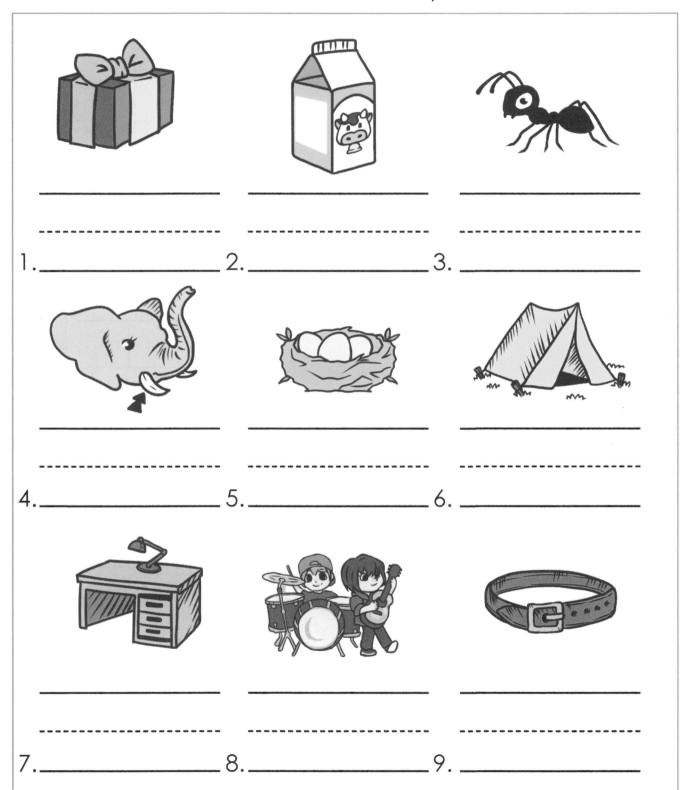

1. _____ 2. _____ 3. _____

4. _____ 5. _____ 6. _____

7. _____ 8. _____ 9. _____

in   it   man   me   21

Write the words for the pictures in the spaces shown by arrows.

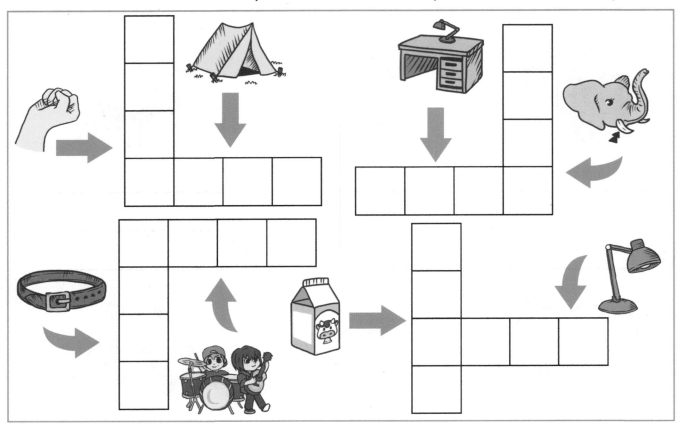

Write the words for the pictures.

1. Mum lost the last . _____

2. The man in the  ran fast. _____

3. The duck sat in the . _____

4. Tim's ![belt] fell off his pants. _____

5. She held the ![milk] in her hand. _____

not   on   one   ran

Tick the sentence that describes the picture.

☐ An ant in sand

☐ An ant in pants.

☐ A belt in a hand.

☐ A belt on the land.

☐ A lamp on my desk.

☐ A lamp in my tent.

☐ Help mum dust.

☐ Help mum lift.

☐ A mask on a man.

☐ A tusk on a man.

☐ Milk on my vest.

☐ Milk in a nest.

saw   three   too   up   (23)

Write the words for the pictures.

1. _____

2. _____

3. _____

4. _____

5. _____

6. _____

Write the words from the box in the space.

| lift | hand | rest | sand | lamp |

1. The cat had a nap in the soft _____ .

2. Dad will help Rick _____ the desk.

3. Ann left the _____ in the tent.

4. Mrs West went to bed for a _____ .

5. Miss Mint had the milk in her _____ .

(24)   watch   you   all   am

Read the words as quickly and accurately as possible.

 Can I read these words?

and	end	bent	bump	ask
band	bend	dent	dump	bask
hand	lend	rent	hump	cask
land	mend	sent	lump	mask
sand	send	tent	pump	task

cast	best	bust	camp	milk
fast	nest	dust	damp	gift
last	rest	gust	lamp	desk
mast	test	must	bond	ant
past	vest	rust	pond	tusk

Time 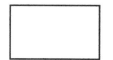  /50 **Right**

Yes I can!

(25)

Say the sounds for these blends.

bl as in

cl as in

fl as in

gl as in

pl as in

sl as in

around   black   but   by

Circle the picture with the blend.

Circle the picture with the blend.

fast   get   going   home

Draw a line to the blend the picture begins with.

cl	cl
gl	bl
pl	sl
fl	cl
pl	bl
gl	sl
bl	pl
cl	fl
pl	gl
pl	gl
sl	cl
cl	fl

Unit 2:5

Circle the blend the picture begins with.

bl cl gl	sl bl cl
fl pl gl	cl bl gl
pl fl sl	sl cl bl
gl pl fl	bl gl cl

(30)   out   was   we   will

Write the missing letters.

_____ ag	_____ ant	_____ ock
_____ ub	_____ ed	_____ ass

Underline the word for the picture.

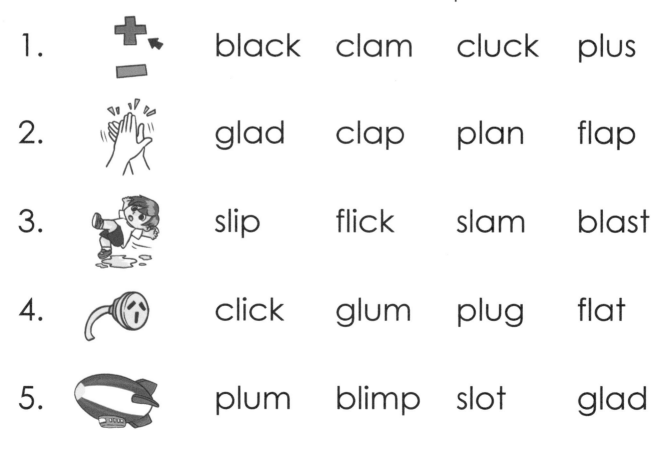

1. black   clam   cluck   plus

2. glad   clap   plan   flap

3. slip   flick   slam   blast

4. click   glum   plug   flat

5. plum   blimp   slot   glad

yellow   yes   an   after   (31)

Write the missing letters.

_ _ _ ap	_ _ _ an	_ _ _ at
_ _ _ uck	_ _ _ ug	_ _ _ ick
_ _ _ ip	_ _ _ um	_ _ _ ap
_ _ _ am	_ _ _ ant	_ _ _ ock

Draw a line to match the words that rhyme.

block	slap	sled	class
clap	plum	glass	bled
glum	slick	plant	slack
flick	clock	black	slant

as   be   brown   cold

Circle the word for the picture.

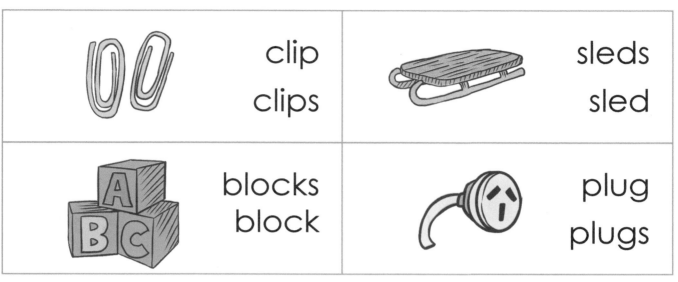

clip
clips

sleds
sled

blocks
block

plug
plugs

List the words with the same letter pattern under each picture.

slim   plan   class   plum   clop

sled   slam   plus   clap

_____   _____   _____

did   ever   fly   from   (33)

Draw a line from the picture to the matching word .

flip
flap
flag

glass
glum
glad

clip
clock
class

slot
slack
sled

Write the word that fits in the word shape box.

plug	flip	block
club	plan	flat
glad	slid	flag
plum	clap	slim

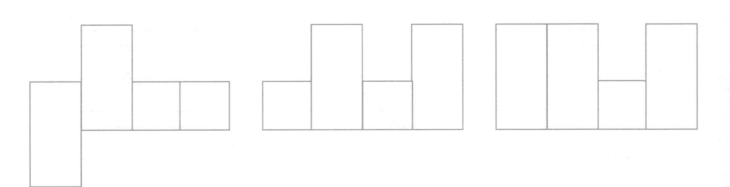

girl   give   had   help

Write the words for the pictures.

1. _____

2. _____

3. _____

4. _____

5. _____

6. _____

7. _____

8. _____

9. _____

her   him   his   if   (35)

Write the words for the pictures in the spaces shown by arrows.

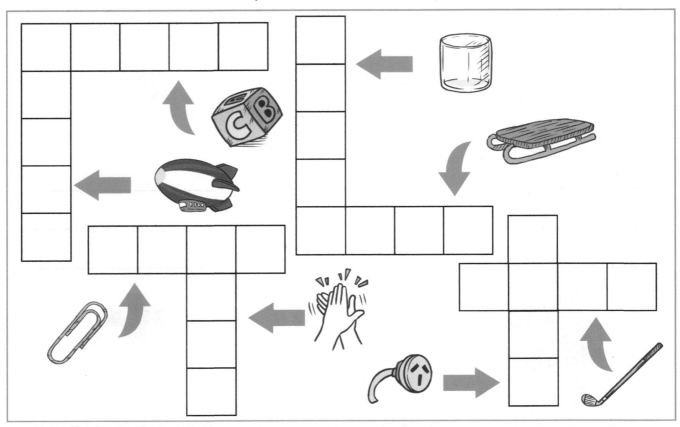

Write the word for the pictures.

1. 'Tick, tock' went the .   _____

2. Did Clem _____ on the rock?   _____

3. Mum held the 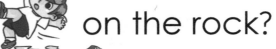 in her hand.   _____

4. The _____ will flap in the wind.   _____

5. She saw the kids on the  .   _____

she   some   stop   two

Tick the sentence that describes the picture.

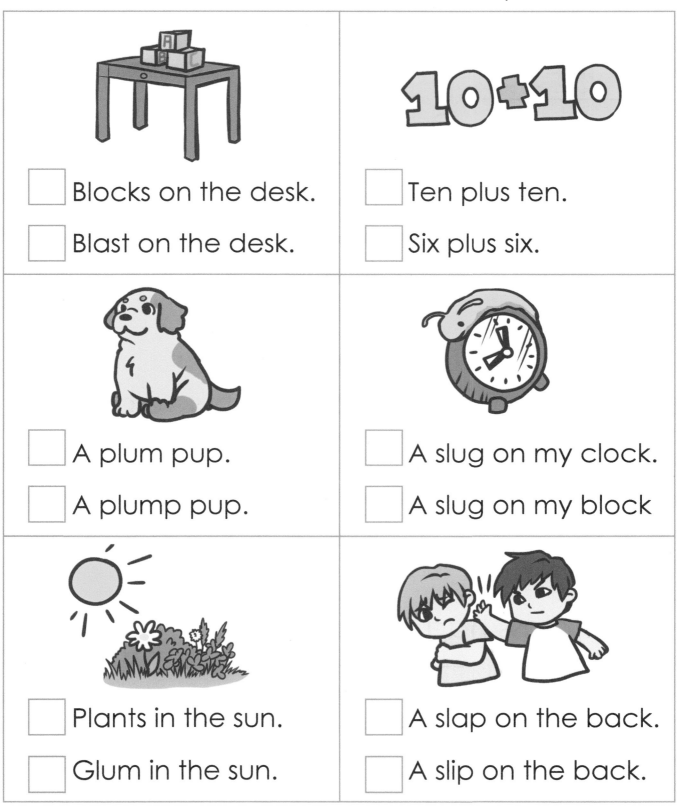

☐ Blocks on the desk.
☐ Blast on the desk.

☐ Ten plus ten.
☐ Six plus six.

☐ A plum pup.
☐ A plump pup.

☐ A slug on my clock.
☐ A slug on my block

☐ Plants in the sun.
☐ Glum in the sun.

☐ A slap on the back.
☐ A slip on the back.

Unit 2:13

Write the words for the pictures.

1. _____

2. _____

3. _____

4. _____

5. _____

6. _____

Write the words for the box in the space.

glad	plus	plug	plums	clock

1. She left ten _____ in the box.

2. Mr Black was _____ to see the sun.

3. The class had to add six _____ six.

4. The black _____ is on the desk.

5. Ask Dad to _____ in the lamp.

(38) gave   got   has   its

Read the words as quickly and accurately as possible.

Can I read these words?

black	clam	clod	glad	plan
bled	clap	clot	glint	plant
blend	clip	clock	glum	plug
bliss	click	club	gloss	plum
block	class	cluck	glass	plus

flab	flip	slam	slid
flag	flit	slap	slim
flap	flick	slack	slip
flat	flop	sled	slick
flax	flock	slept	stop

Time     40   **Right**

Yes I can!

(39)

Say the sounds for these blends.

sc as in 	st as in
sk as in 	sw as in 
sm as in 	tw as in 
sn as in 	fr as in 
sp as in 	scr as in 
str as in 	

know   let   live   made

Circle the picture with the blend.

sc

sk

sm

sn

sp

str

st

sw

Circle the picture with the blend.

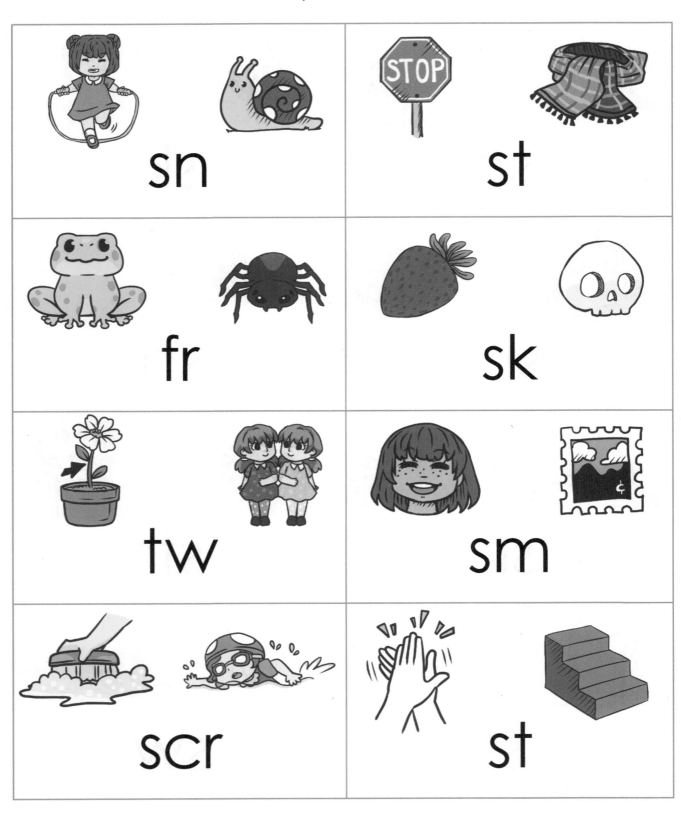

over   put   round   school

Draw a line to the blend the picture begins with.

sk	sp
sm	str
sn	st
fr	st
tw	sn
sw	sp
tw	str
scr	scr
sc	tw
sm	fr
sn	sk
sp	sw

so   soon   ten   that   43

Circle the blend the picture begins with.

sc sk sm	sw fr tw
str scr sp	sk sm sn
st sw fr	scr str sc
sn sp st	scr str tw

under   your   about   again

© 2022 Hunter Calder and Five Senses Education Pty Ltd

Write the missing letters.

_ _ _ amp	_ _ _ og	_ _ _ im
_ _ _ ip	_ _ _ op	_ _ _ ull

Underline the word that matches the picture

1. steps   scab   skin   smog

2. snap   stand   swell   spot

3. frost   stem   scrub   swift

4. strap   stop   skid   scat

5. snug   stump   spill   twin

always   any   ask   ate   45

Write the missing letters.

___ ___ ___ et	___ ___ ___ ick	___ ___ ___ ell
___ ___ ___ ill	___ ___ ___ ump	___ ___ ___ in
___ ___ ___ ost	___ ___ ___ ack	___ ___ ___ eck
___ ___ ___ ock	___ ___ ___ ill	___ ___ ___ un

Draw a line to match the words that rhyme.

scan	scamp	stiff	smack
smell	spin	stack	scrub
stamp	span	stub	spill
twin	spell	skill	sniff

(46) cannot   could   does   father

Circle the word for the picture.

	frogs frog		stamp stamps
	scrub scrubs		twins twin

List the words with the same word pattern
under each picture.

swam   skin   stack   stick   swift

skill   swell   skim   still

_____

- - - - - - - - - - - - - - -

_____

- - - - - - - - - - - - - - -

_____

- - - - - - - - - - - - - - -

_____

first   found   how   long   47

Draw a line from the picture to the matching word.

stick
step
stamp

swell
swim
swept

stop
stuck
stun

skull
skim
skill

Write the word that fits in the word shape box.

smell   fret   scrub

snug   frost   spell

smack   twin   spot

scan   twig   spend

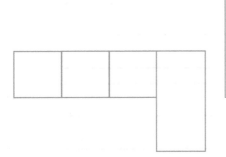

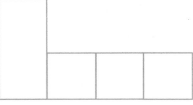

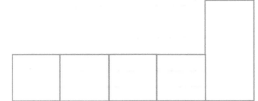

48   or   them   then   they

© 2022 Hunter Calder and Five Senses Education Pty Ltd

Write the words for the pictures.

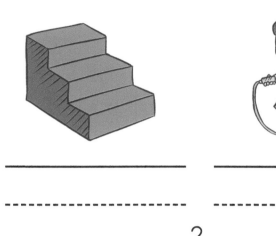

1. _____   2. _____   3. _____

4. _____   5. _____   6. _____

7. _____   8. _____   9. _____

walk   went   were   what   (49)

Write the words for the pictures in the spaces shown by arrows.

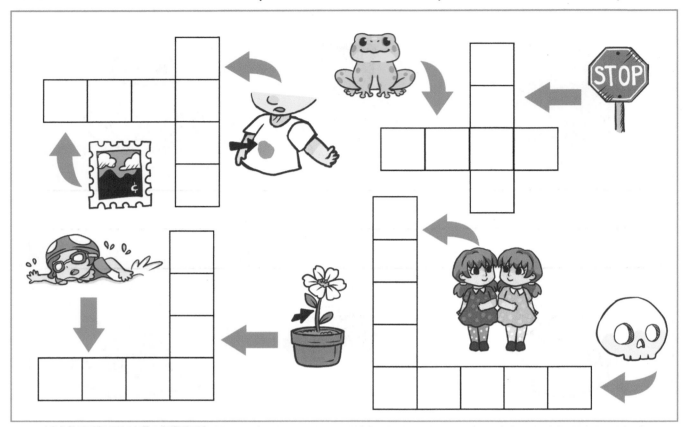

Write the word for the pictures.

1. Mrs Frost swept the  . _____

2. The dog sat on the  . _____

3. The 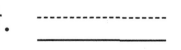 of the plant was bent. _____

4. The swam in the pond. _____

5. Stan has ten in his hand. _____

50 when   with   because   been

Tick the sentence that describes the picture.

☐ Fran is slim.

☐ Fran is a stem.

☐ A frog on a stump.

☐ A frog on a stamp.

☐ Stick in the mud.

☐ Stand in the mud.

☐ Spots on my top.

☐ Spin my top.

☐ A smack on my hand.

☐ A snack in my hand.

☐ I spell 'stop'.

☐ I spell 'stock'.

before   bring   children   done   (51)

Write the words for the pictures.

1. _____	2. _____	3. _____
4. _____	5. _____	6. _____

Write the words for the box in the space.

stuck	still	swam	snug	scrub

1. Fred _____ past the kids on the dock.

2. The bus got _____ in the soft sand.

3. Mum will _____ the spot off Tom's pants.

4. The class sat _____ at their desks.

5. The twins are _____ as a bug in a rug.

52 every   goes   mother   much

Read the words as quickly and accurately as possible

 Can I read these words?

scab	skid	smog	snap	spit
scan	skin	smug	snip	spot
scat	skip	smack	snug	spell
scamp	skill	smell	snack	spill
scant	skull	smock	sniff	spend

stem	stop	swam	fret	scrap
step	stock	swim	frog	scrub
stamp	stuck	swell	frost	scruff
stick	stuff	swept	twig	strap
still	stump	swift	twin	strip

Time [   ]    /40   **Right**

Yes I can!   (53)

Say the sounds for these blends.

br as in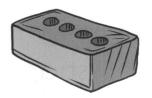

cr as in

dr as in

gr as in

pr as in

tr as in

nk as in

must   never   once   open

Circle the picture with the blend.

br	**cr**
dr	**gr**
pr	**tr**
nk	**dr**

our   say   take   tell

Circle the picture with the blend.

cr

nk

dr

tr

pr

gr

nk

br

there   upon   us   want

Draw a line to the blend the picture begins or ends with.

(drum)	cr dr gr	(bunk bed)	nk br cr
(grass)	tr pr gr	(cross)	cr br nk
(brick)	cr br tr	(prince)	pr gr dr
(hand dropping)	cr gr dr	(truck)	nk tr dr

wish   would   brother   buy   57

Circle the blend the picture begins or ends with.

cr dr gr	pr tr nk
dr cr br	pr nk br
cr br gr	tr pr gr
cr dr gr	nk br cr

(58)   draw   drink   even   fall

Write the missing letters.

_ _ _ ick	_ _ _ ess	_ _ _ uck
_ _ _ ab	_ _ _ ass	_ _ _ op

Underline the word that matches the picture

1.  brag   cram   drum   drip

2. cross   grin   press   trick

3.  pink   tank   bran   trust

4.  junk   trip   grab   wink

5.  sink   bunk   crib   brat

grow   hold   hot   just   59

Write the missing letters.

si _ _ _	_ _ _ ip	_ _ _ ap
cla _ _ _	_ _ _ um	_ _ _ im
ba _ _ _	_ _ _ ag	_ _ _ ust
tru _ _ _	_ _ _ op	_ _ _ ip

Draw a line to match the words that rhyme.

grass	press	crack	trunk
bank	brass	junk	trick
trim	drank	drop	track
dress	grim	brick	prop

keep   only   pull   show

Circle the word for the picture.

cross	tank
crosses	tanks
trucks	drums
truck	drum

List the words with the same word pattern
under each picture.

grab   brag   cram   grin   grip
crop   brass   cross   bran

the   too   was   why   61

Unit 4:9

Draw a line from the picture to the matching word.

drink
dress
drop

sink
junk
bunk

bran
brick
brag

cross
cram
crack

Write the word that fits in the word shape box.

crop	grip	trick
trap	prod	blink
blink	trip	tank
trick	grin	clank

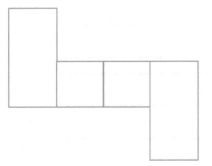

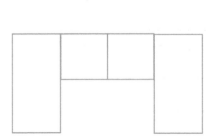

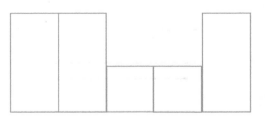

(62)   think   those   very   where

Write the words for the pictures.

1 _____

2 _____

3 _____

4 _____

5 _____

6 _____

7 _____

8 _____

9 _____

which   work   best   better   63

© 2022 Hunter Calder and Five Senses Education Pty Ltd

Write the words for the pictures in the spaces shown by arrows.

Write the words for the pictures.

1. Can you jump off the bed?

----

2. Brett left the bricks on the  .

----

3. Dad got the out of the trunk.

----

4. It was too wet to cut the .

----

5. The ink fell on Mum best .

----

(64) both   clean   cut   eight

Tick the sentence that describes the picture.

☐ A big stink.
☐ A big wink.

☐ Cut the grass.
☐ Cut the brass.

☐ Fran's best dress.
☐ Fran's best press.

☐ Drop the blink.
☐ Drop the drink.

☐ A rat in a track.
☐ A rat in a trap.

☐ A tramp with a sack.
☐ A tramp with a rack.

five   four   full   light   65

Write the words for the pictures.

1. _____

2. _____

3. _____

4. _____

5. _____

6. _____

Write the words from the box in the space.

sink   crab   drum   junk   dress

1. The drink was next to the _____ .

2. Fran has a rip in her pink _____ .

3. The tracks of the _____ are in the sand.

4. Greg left the _____ on the truck.

5. The _____ went 'rat-a-tat-tat'.

(66)   myself   off   pick   please

Read the words as quickly and accurately as possible

Can I read these words?

brag	crab	drag	grab	pram
bran	crack	dress	grin	press
brat	crib	drip	grip	prim
brick	crop	drop	gruff	prod
brass	cross	drum	grass	prop

trap	bank	ink	bunk
track	blank	blink	clunk
trip	crank	drink	junk
trick	sank	pink	sunk
truck	tank	wink	trunk

Time     40   **Right**

Yes I can!

More work
with blends

pretty   read   shall   six

Unit 5:2

Write the missing letters.

_ _ _ im	wi _ _ _	gi _ _ _
_ _ _ ab	_ _ _ ant	_ _ _ amp

Underline the word for the picture.

1.   help   flag   strap   grin

2.   black   frost   hand   junk

3.   next   plum   trick   stump

4.   cost   skid   spot   glum

5.   tent   sled   spill   drip

today   try   use   well   69

Unit 5:3

Write the missing letters.

bu _ _ _

ca _ _ _

li _ _ _

lu _ _ _

_ _ _ am

_ _ _ ock

_ _ _ uck

_ _ _ ip

_ _ _ ep

_ _ _ ick

_ _ _ and

_ _ _ ock

Draw a line to match the words that rhyme

nest	swell	slip	band
clap	blink	land	flip
spell	vest	twin	drop
sink	flap	crop	spin

(70)   why   write   baby   daughter

Circle the word for the picture.

	hands hand		drum drums
	truck trucks		blocks block

List the words with the same letter pattern under each picture.

blank   sank   drip   slap   drum

slot   drop   slim   crank

far   house   hurt   kind   71

Unit 5:5

Draw a line from the picture to the matching word.

tent
went
bent

still
stick
stem

class
click
clip

frost
frog
fret

Write the word that fits in the word shape box.

glass	drink	lump
pond	black	camp
press	brick	flag
gift	bless	trim

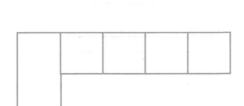
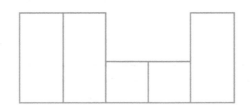
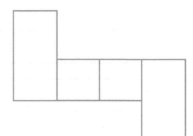

(72)   laugh   Mr   Mrs   own

Write the words for the pictures.

1. _____

2. _____

3. _____

4. _____

5. _____

6. _____

7. _____

8. _____

9. _____

right   seven   sing   sister   ⟨73⟩

Write the words for the pictures in the spaces shown by arrows.

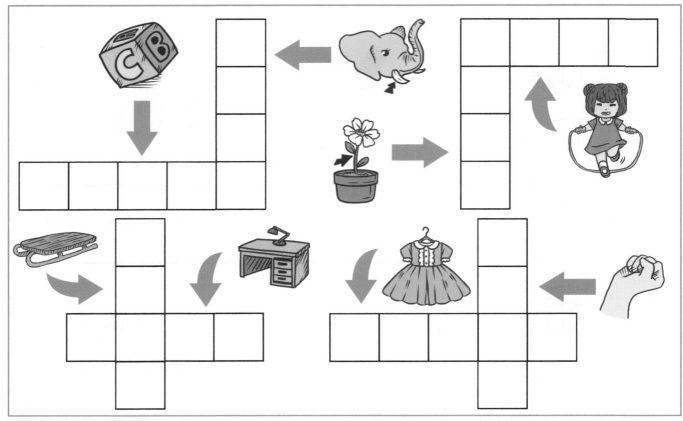

Write the words for the pictures.

1. Ann had a of milk. _____

2. The twins ran up the . _____

3. The  is on the desk. _____

4. He left the plants in the . _____

5. Fran ran with the . _____

(74)   sleep   something   son   start

Tick the sentence that describes the picture.

I stand on a stump.

A band on a stump.

Snug in the red.

Snug in my bed.

Flip on the steps.

Trip on the steps.

Bend the dress.

Mend the dress.

Sit still at my desk.

Sit still in my nest.

Frog on the sled.

Frost on the sled.

thank   together   warm   75

Write the words for the pictures.

1. _____	2. _____	3. _____
4. _____	5. _____	6. _____

Write the words from the box in the space.

lamp	nest	plus	scrub	stump

1. The hen in the _____ went 'cluck, cluck'.

2. Brad had to plug in the _____ .

3. What is ten _____ ten?

4. Tess has to _____ the spot on her dress.

5. The black dog sat on the _____ .

(76) wash   water   white

Read the words as quickly and accurately as possible

 ## Can I read these words?

hand	cross	smell	grip
black	mend	dress	snug
scamp	clam	sent	lump
brick	skin	glad	plus
press	strap	flat	milk
truck	swim	drink	camp
stem	flock	slap	slip
flag	fast	dust	sunk
mast	bank	frog	scrap
pond	gift	tusk	wink

Time   /40 **Right**

Yes I can!

(77)

Achievement Tests

The Five Senses Phonics Achievement Tests complement each book in the Five Senses Phonics series. They are specifically designed to enable teachers to ensure that what has been taught remains current in the student's repertoire of skills. They can then identify areas that need reteaching or reinforcement.

The format of each Five Senses Phonics Achievement Test is identical to the equivalent book so students encounter activities with which they are familiar. Each test evaluates skills and sight words students have been taught. The careful design of the tests, ensures that the monitoring of progress is a positive and non-threatening exercise.

For ease of administration, the tests are photocopiable. The class record sheets and student record sheets allow the teacher to scan student performance on an individual or whole class basis. Taken as a group, the tests give a running record of each student's skill acquisition of the phonic hierarchy. Teachers who teach reading systematically and record student progress methodically will find the Five Senses Phonics First Achievement Tests an indispensable part of their teaching routine.

How to use these tests

The Five Senses Phonics Achievement Tests are intended to be an encouraging record of progress, not an intimidating assessment. The tests can be administered to individual students or the entire class. Allow approximately 30 minutes to complete each test.

Each group of tests contains one or two sight vocabulary tests. If administering the test to the class as a whole, have individual students read groups of sight words, then ask the class to read all sight words together. Keep watch for children who are having trouble, and test them later individually.

Maintain a positive attitude while administering the tests, and reward success with stickers, stamps and merit certificates. To attain mastery students should obtain at least 80 marks out of a possible 100. Any areas in the Test that indicate weakness should be retaught and then reinforced.

Test Record Sheet

Student .... Date..

Page	Test		
80	1	Word completion; word recognition	/11
81	2	Singular-plural; recognising word patterns	/13
82	3	Word recognition; word shape boxes	/ 7
83	4	Spelling initial and terminal blends	/ 9
84	5	Crossword puzzles; sentence completion	/ 9
85	6	Sentence comprehension	/ 6
86	7	Singular-plural spelling; sentence completion	/11
87	8	Reading initial and terminal blends	/34

Knowledge of initial and terminal blends   **Total**   /100

.   9   **Basic sight vocabulary**   /40

Test 4:1

Word recognition; word shape boxes

Write the missing letters.

_ _ _ ha_ _ _	_ _ _ _ _ _ ed	_ _ _ _ _ _ ip
_ _ _ _ _ _ og	_ _ _ _ _ _ ass	_ _ _ wi _ _ _

Underline the word that matches the picture

1.   snug   stump   spill   skin

2.   next   cost   nest   bump

3.   glass   clap   plant   flat

4.   spot   step   twin   frost

5.   sink   trip   press   cross

Score ☐ / 11

Test 4:2   Singular-plural; recognising word patterns

Circle the word for the picture.

tent tents	frog frogs
truck trucks	block blocks

List the words with the same letter pattern under each picture.

plan   swam   brass   plum   brag

swell   plus   bran   swept

Test 4:3

Draw a line from the picture to the matching word.

sand
band
land

step
stop
stamp

bunk
junk
trunk

drift
dress
drum

Write the word that fits in the word shape box.

pest	scrub	trap
bent	smell	grin
help	smack	tank
pump	spend	prod

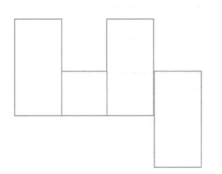

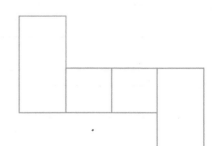

Score / 7

Test 4:4

Spelling initial and terminal blends

Write the words for the pictures.

1. _____
2. _____
3. _____

4. _____
5. _____
6. _____

7. _____
8. _____
9. _____

Score ☐ / 9

Test 4:5

Crossword puzzles; sentence completion

Write the words for the pictures in the spaces shown by arrow

Write the words for the pictures.

1. Mum left the in the sink. _____

2. Mr Black had to stop his  . _____

3. Frank scrubs the back . _____

4. Spot the dog slept on the  . _____

5. Did Mrs Frost spill milk on her  ? _____

 84

Score ☐ / 9

Test 4:6

Sentence comprehension

Tick the sentence that describes the picture.

☐ I must help Mum lift.

☐ I must help Mum dust.

☐ A flap on my back.

☐ A slap on my back.

☐ Fran spells 'stop'.

☐ Fran spells 'step'.

☐ In my best mess.

☐ In my best dress.

☐ A big frog on a truck.

☐ A big frog on a stump.

☐ I can cut the grass.

☐ I can cut the class.

Score ☐ / 6

85

Test 4:7

Singular-plural spelling; sentence completion

Write the words for the pictures.

1. _____	2. _____	3. _____
4. _____	5. _____	6. _____

Write the words from the box in the space.

desk   scrub   truck   past   plus

1. I can add ten _____ six.

2. Dad left the stamps in his _____ .

3. Mum will _____ the spot on my dress.

4. Glen ran _____ the kids on the steps.

5. The _____ was stuck in the soft sand.

(86)   **Score** [/11]

Test 4:8

Read the words as quickly and accurately as possible

band	scat	smell	grip
spill	rest	dress	snug
cross	still	sent	lump
camp	junk	glad	plus
ant	tusk		

brick	slim	swim	glad
gift	snap	frog	strip
block	dress	flat	prop
skip	trap	plus	trim

Score | /34

Test 4:9

Basic Sight vocabulary

Read these sight words as quickly and accurately as possible.

watch	too	around	do
you	one	black	came
am	saw	call	fast
up	ran	by	get
all	three	but	eat

make	be	help	know
no	as	him	many
into	after	some	school
home	girl	two	your
going	did	did	under

(88)

Score [/40]